What Do You See?

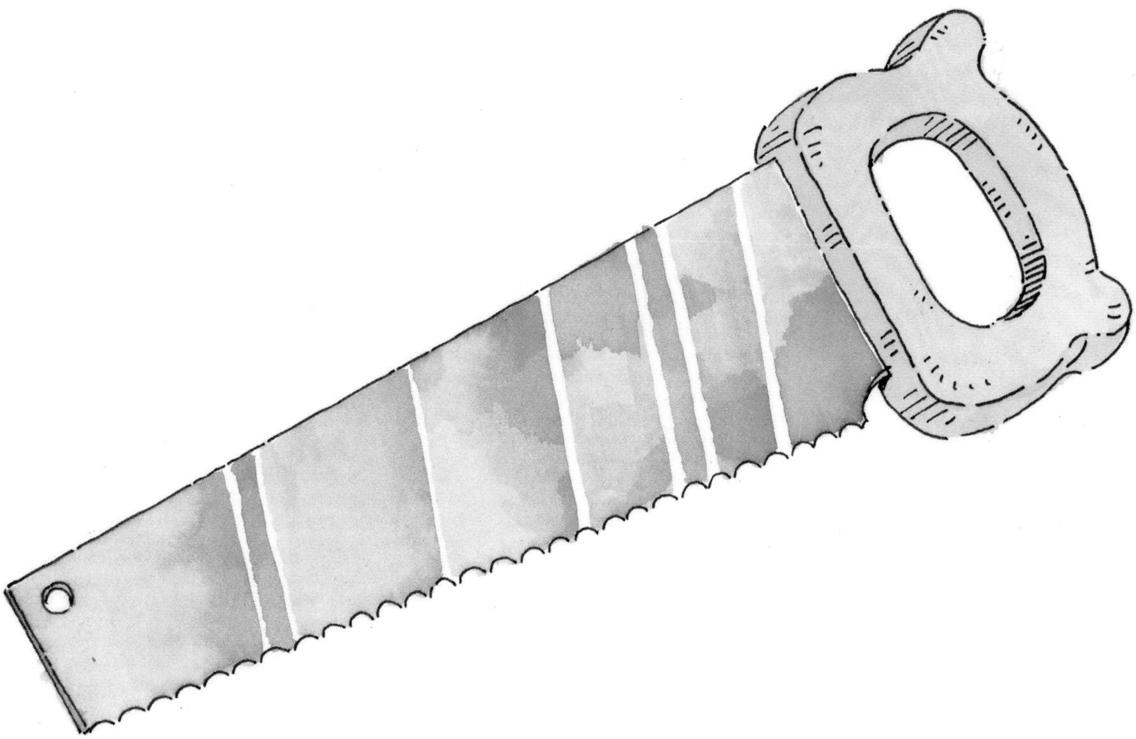

Hannah Barthel
Illustrations by George Ulrich

HAMPTON-BROWN

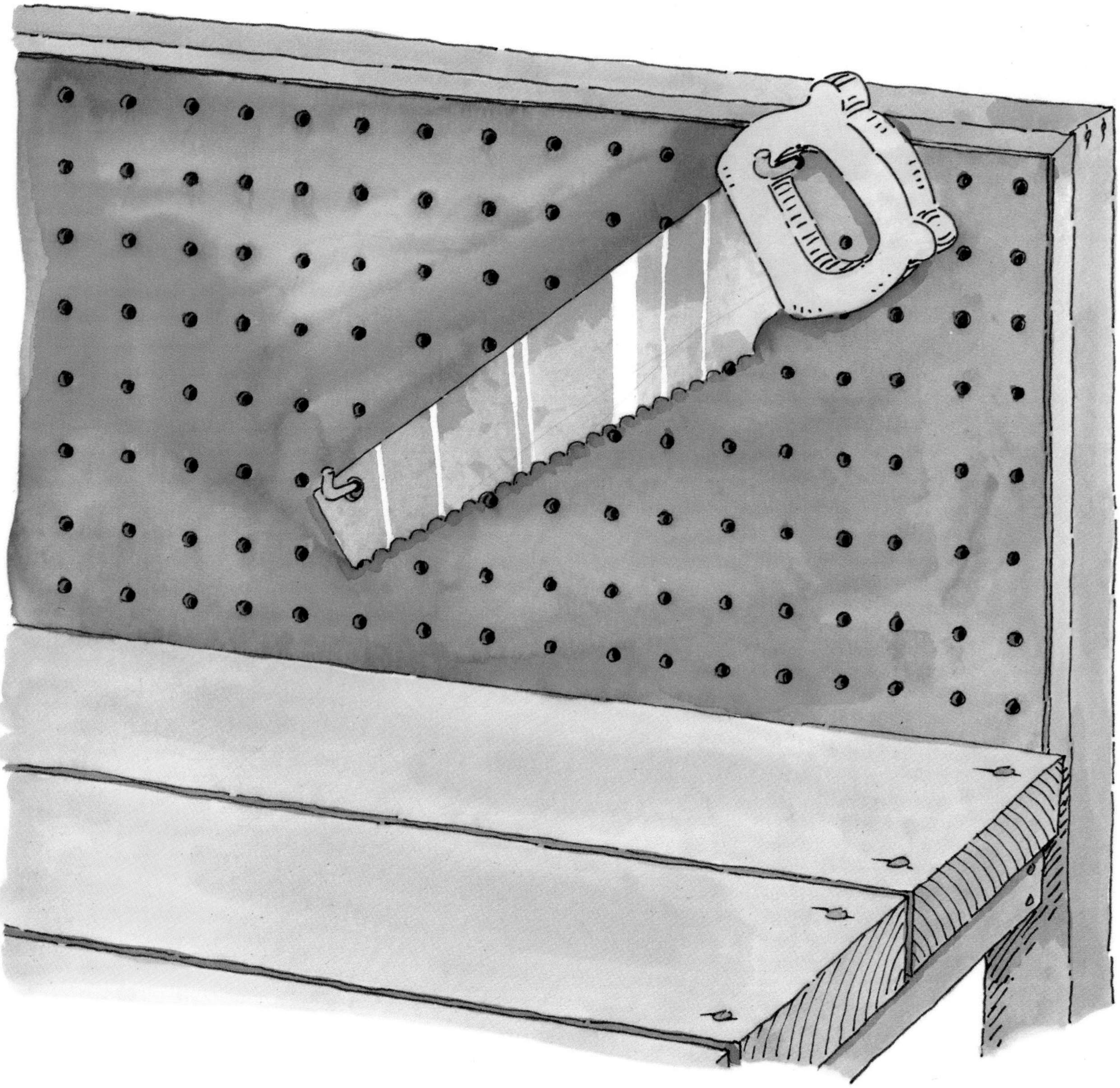

I see a saw.

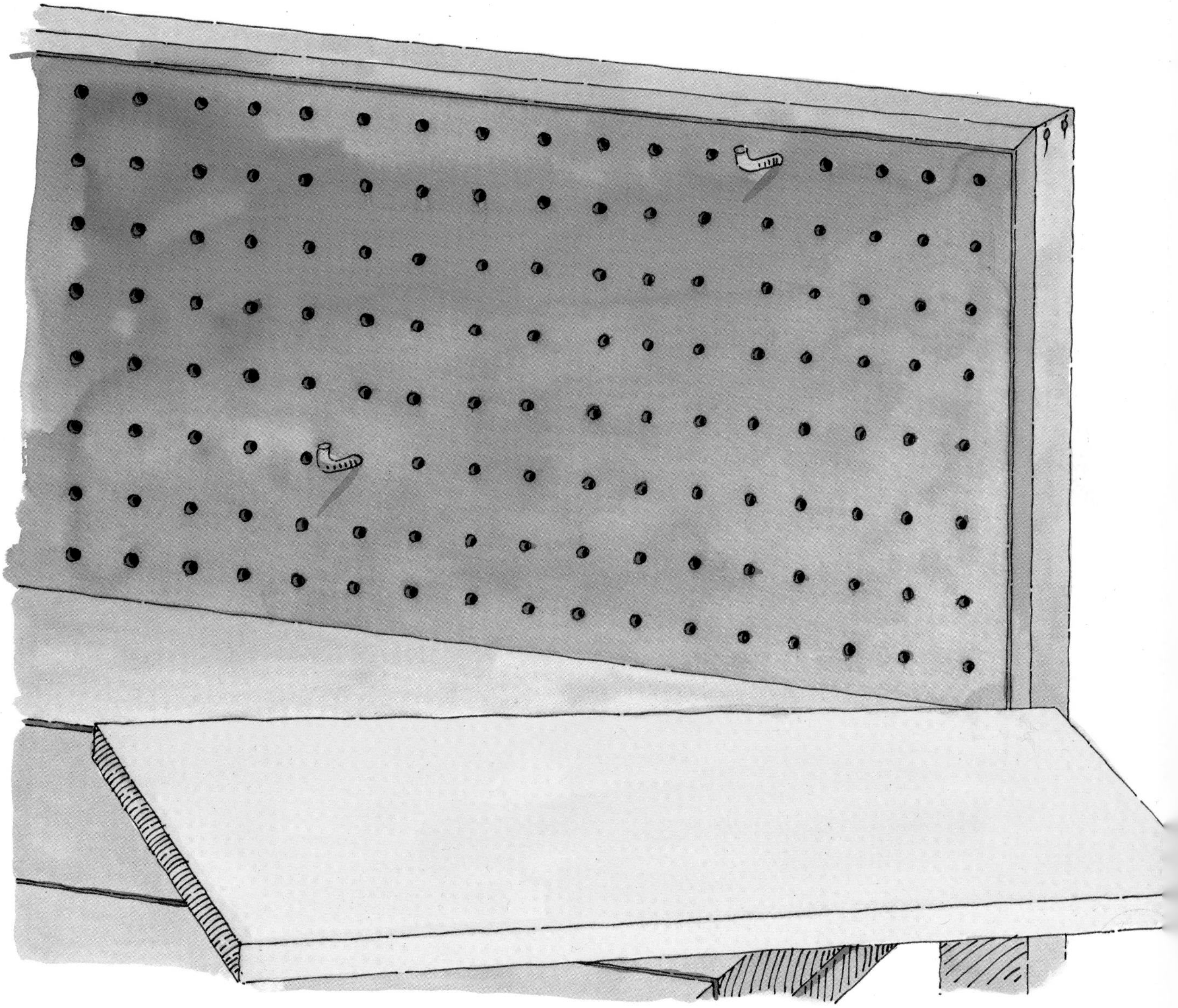

I see a board.

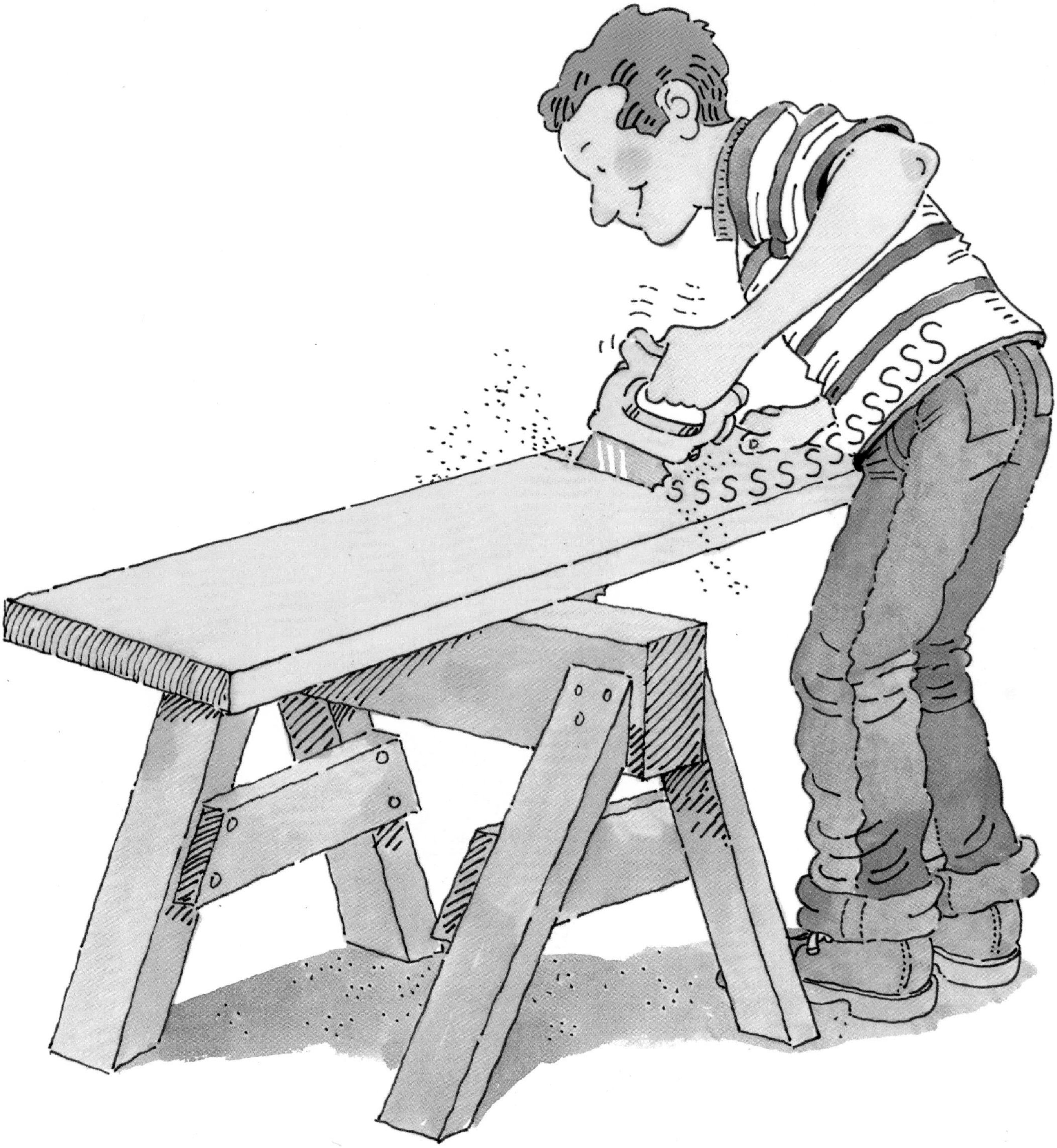
SSSSSSSSSSSSSS

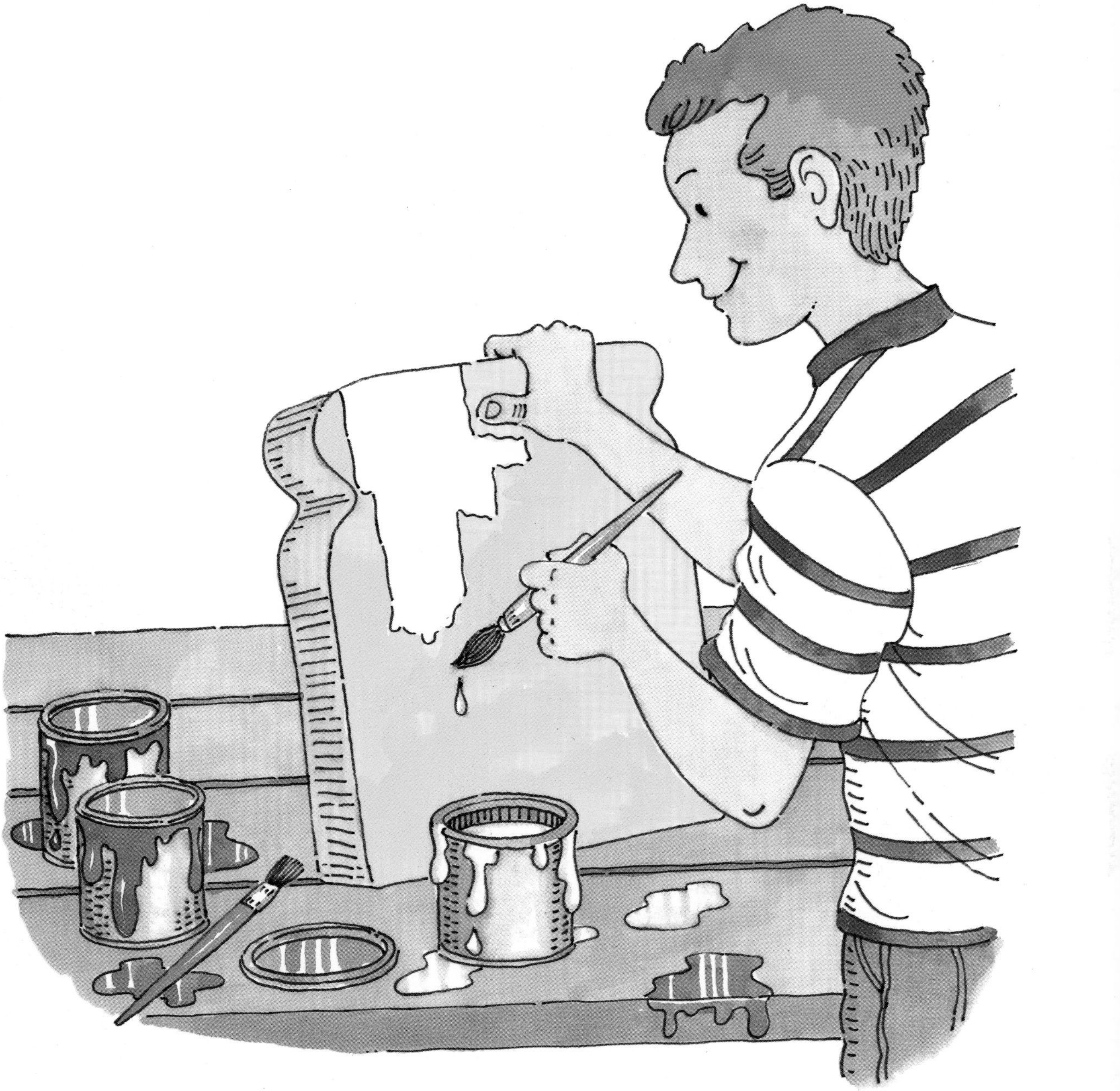

I see paint.

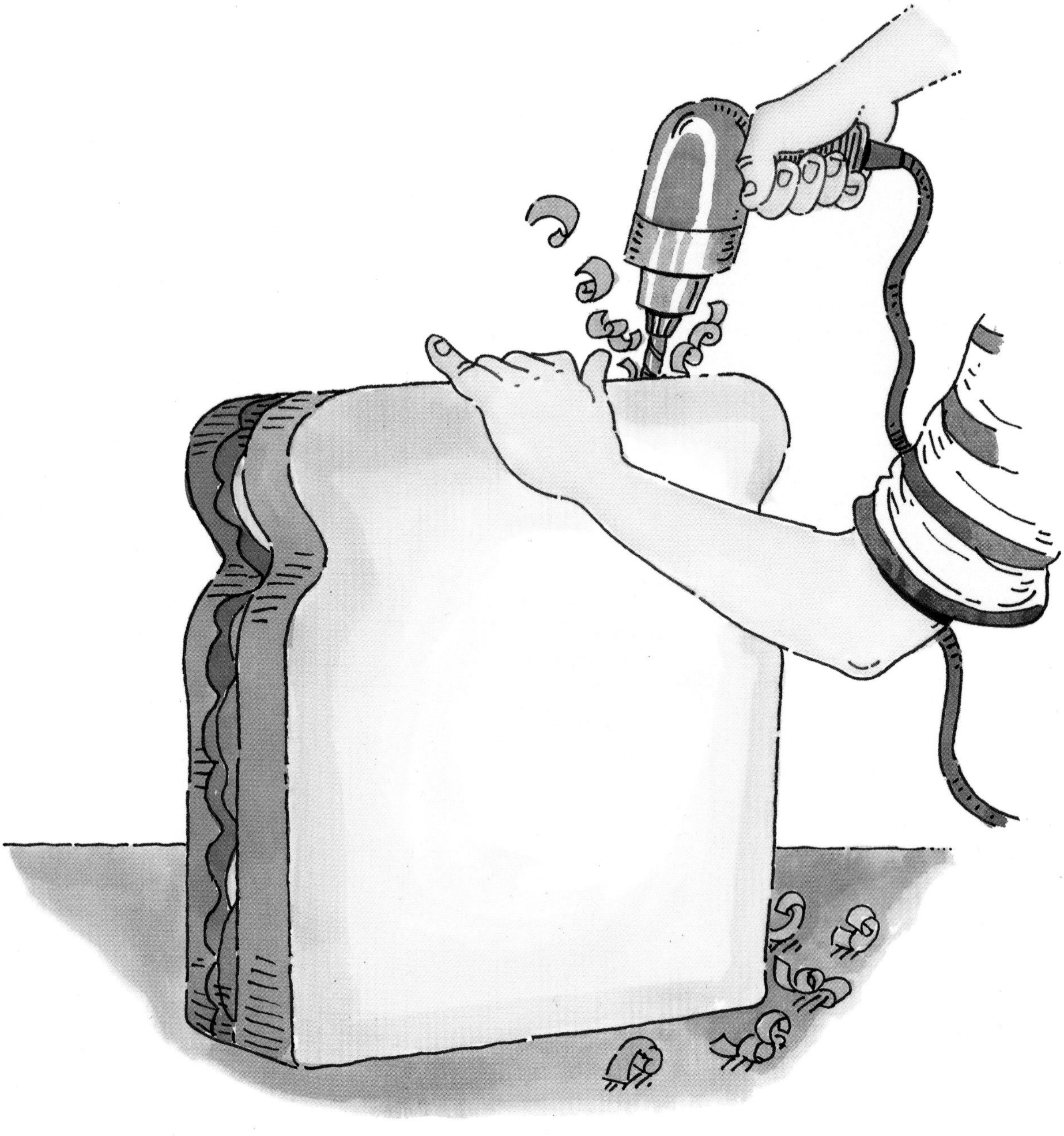

I see a sandwich.

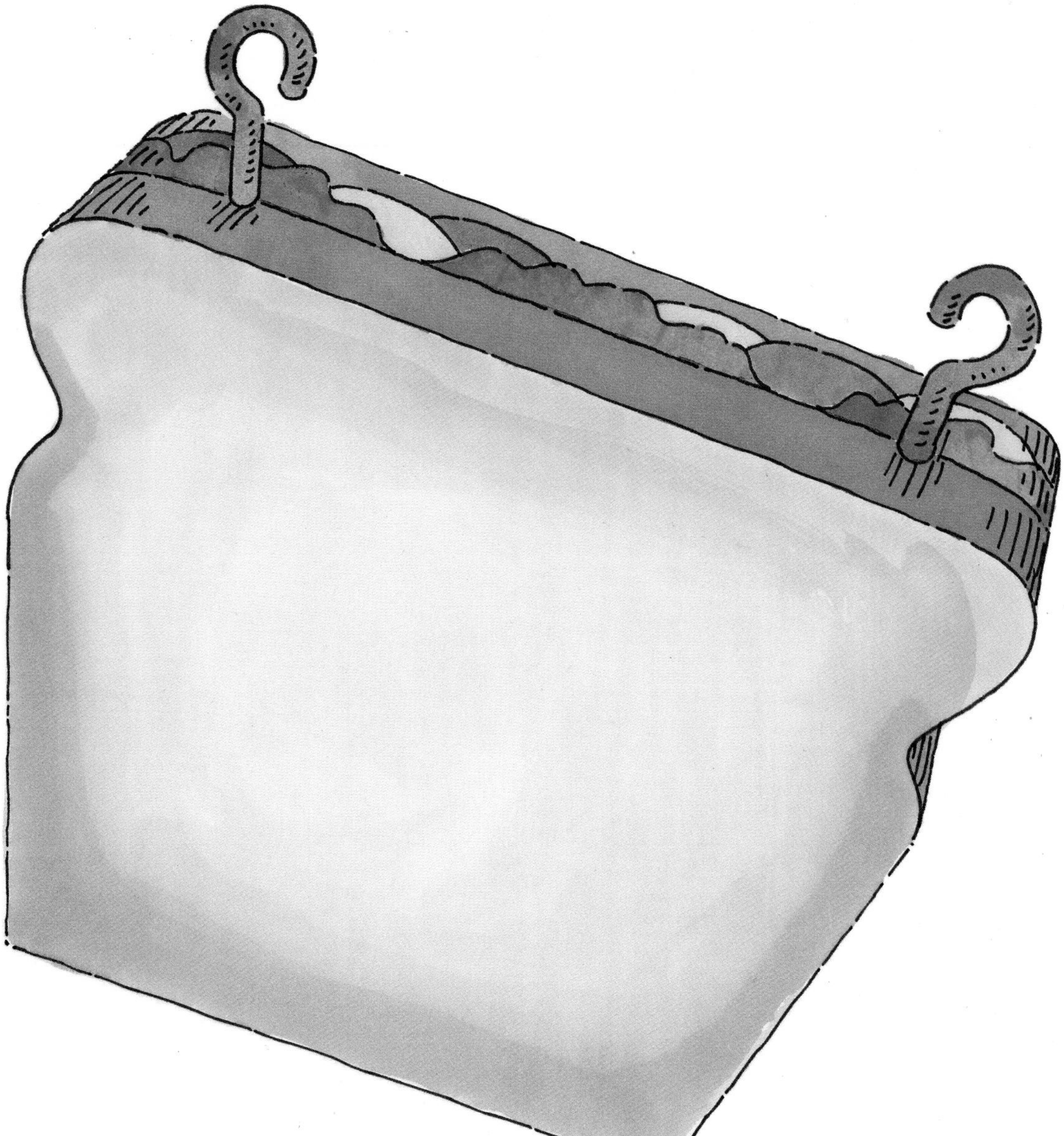

I see hooks.

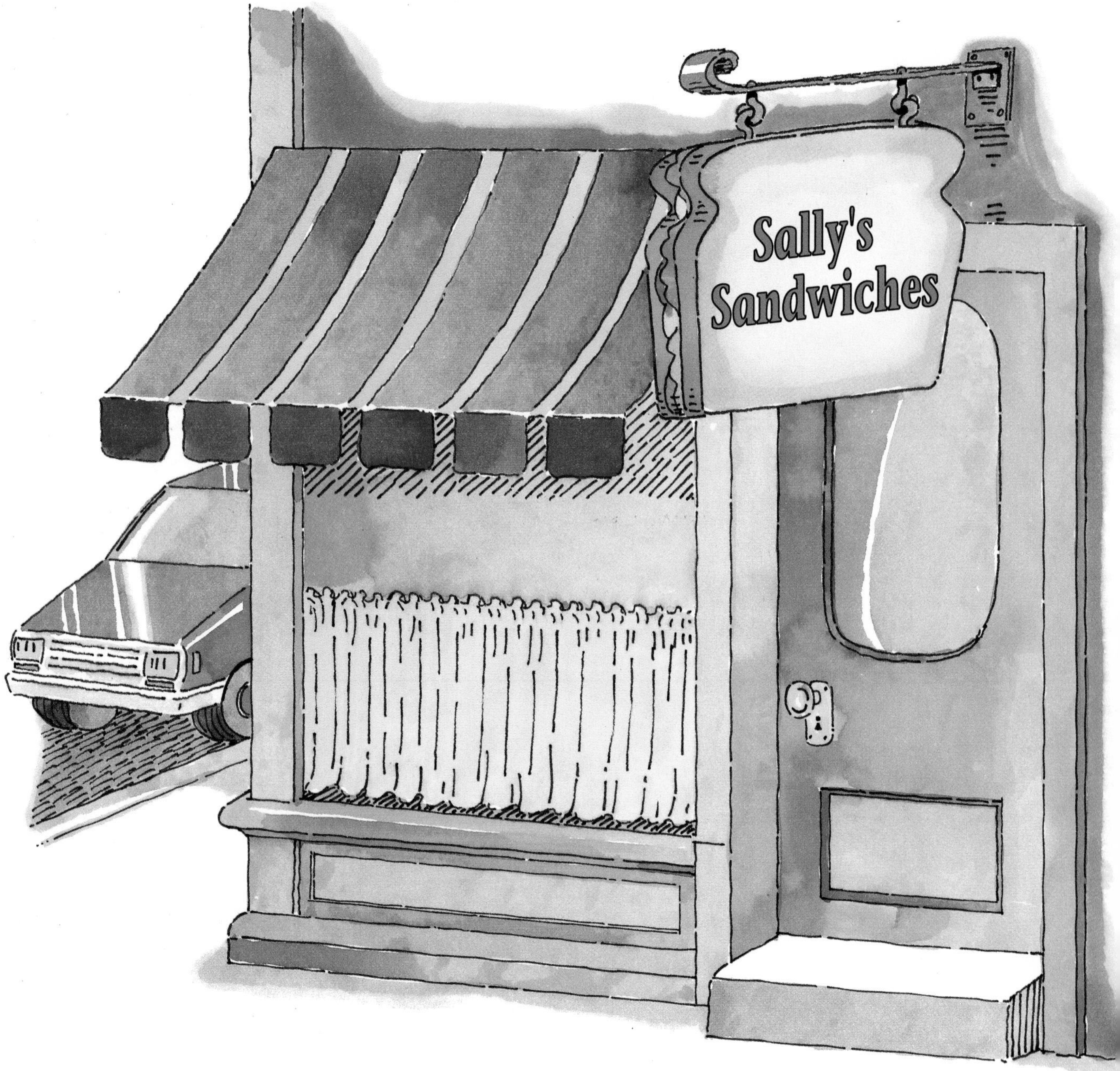

I see a sign.